CW00855154

PICTURE CREDITS

BIOS 41 Norbert Wu; 56 Seistre; 57 h Seistre; 57 b Alain Compost; 82 Daniel Heuclin; 83 Michel. BRUCE COLEMAN 13 Jane Burton; 21 Hermann Brehm; 48 Robert Maier; 55 Rod Williams; 60 Jane Burton; 87 John Cancalosi. JACANA Jacana/PHR J. Lepore; 14 Michel Loup; 17 Jacques Poulard; 19 Nobert Wu; 22, Jacana/PHR, Ochocki; 23 Jean-Maris Bassot; 24 Jacana/PHR, N. Smythe; 25 John Sundance; 26 Martial Colas; 27 Yves Lanceau ; 30, 31 Michel Luquet; 32, 33 Armelle Kerneis-Dragesco; 36, 37 Jacana/PHR Merlin Tuttle; 40 Norbert Wu; 44 Jacana/PHR Paul A. Zahl; 46 Nobert Wu; 47 Alain Devez; 47 Jacana/PHR Merlin Tuttle; 49 Jacana/PHR R. Austing; 50, 51 Michel Luquet; 53 Rudolf Konig; 58 Varin/Visage; 59 Jacques Robert; 61 Jacana/PHR Mc Hugh; 66, 67 John Cancalosi ; 68 Jacana/PHR J Lepore; 69 Varin/Visage; 70, 71 Eric Janini; 74 Rouxaime; 75 Herbert Schwind; 78 Nobert Wu; 79 Jacana PHR L Naylor; 81 b Jacana/PHR Rod Planck; 85 h Alain Rainon; 85 b Axel; 86 Jean-Philippe Varin ; 88 John Cancalosi ; 90 Rudolf Konig. FOTOGRAM-STONE 11 Mike Severns ; 16 Art Wolfe ; 20 Art Wolfe. PIX Couverture Maris Clay; 18 Pix/Planet Earth Peter David; 39 Pix/Planet Earth Pete Oxford; 52 Pix/Planet Earth Brian Kenney. OXFORD SCIENTIFIC FILM 4 Clive Bromhall; 64 David Haring; 4eme de couverture Clive Bromhall. SUNSET 12 Sunset/NHPA; 15 Sunset/Silvestris Konrad Wothe ; 28 Mc Donald;29 Sunset/ANT; 34 Sunset/Silvestris Fritz Frenzel; 35 Sunset/Silvestris R.D. Mackay; 38 Gérard Lacz; 42, 43 Sunset/Animals Animals; 54 Sunset/NHPA; 65 Sunset/Silvestris Wolgang Lummer; 72 Sunset/Slivestris Frieder Sauer; 73 Sunset/NHPA; 76 Sunset/Animals Animals; 77 Sunset/ANT; 80, 81 h Sunset/Animals Animals; 84 Géard Lacs ; 89 Sunset/FLPA.

CONSULTANTS

Martine Desoutter, Roger Bour and Michel Tranier, The Natural History Museum, Paris.

EDITOR

Polly Goodman

Text copyright © 2000 Hodder Wayland
French edition © 1998 Éditions Mango

First published in France in 1998 by Éditions Mango. This edition published in 2000 by Hodder Wayland, an imprint of Hodder Children's Books.

All rights reserved. No part of this publication may be reproduced, stored in a retrieval system, or transmitted, in any form or by any means without the prior written permission of the publisher, nor be otherwise circulated in any form of binding or cover other than that in which it is published and without a similar condition being imposed on the subsequent purchaser.

A Catalogue record for this book is available from the British Library.

ISBN 0 7502 2876 8

Printed in China.

Hodder Children's Books
A division of Hodder Headline plc
338 Euston Road, London NW1 3BH

BIZARRE BEASTS

A closer look at some of the world's strangest-looking creatures

BÉATRICE FONTANEL

Wayland

Am imprint of Hodder Children's Books

HOW BIZARRE!

Prepare to meet some of the most bizarre-looking species on earth! Over the next 84 pages, you will be introduced to a parade of nature's wierdest animals, chosen for their strange appearances. Have you ever seen creatures with transparent bellies, fingers like humans or tongues like sandpaper? Some, like the deep-sea viperfish, have luminous bodies which glow in the dark. Others, like the chameleon, can change colour according to their mood. Meet the male anglerfish that attaches himself to a female's skin with his jaws and hangs on for life. Discover creatures that can swallow prey much bigger than themselves, stretching their jaws and stomachs out of all proportion.

But why are these creatures so bizarre? Look closer and you will find that each unusual shape or colour has a special purpose. Each creature is cleverly adapted for survival and their strange appearances help them in different ways.

methods of self-defence are used, such as poisonous substances and body armour. Compare the different ways of finding and catching food, and look at how each species is specially suited to its own habitat, whether it is rainforest, desert or ocean.

Each spread in this book features a different bizarre beast. At the top of each spread, the creature's scientific name is shown in coloured capitals, with its English name underneath. The main information section describes each animal's distinguishing features and how it lives its daily life. In the right-hand column, at-a-glance facts show where it is found in the world, its habitat, size and diet.

▼ *The three-horned chameleon.*

CONT

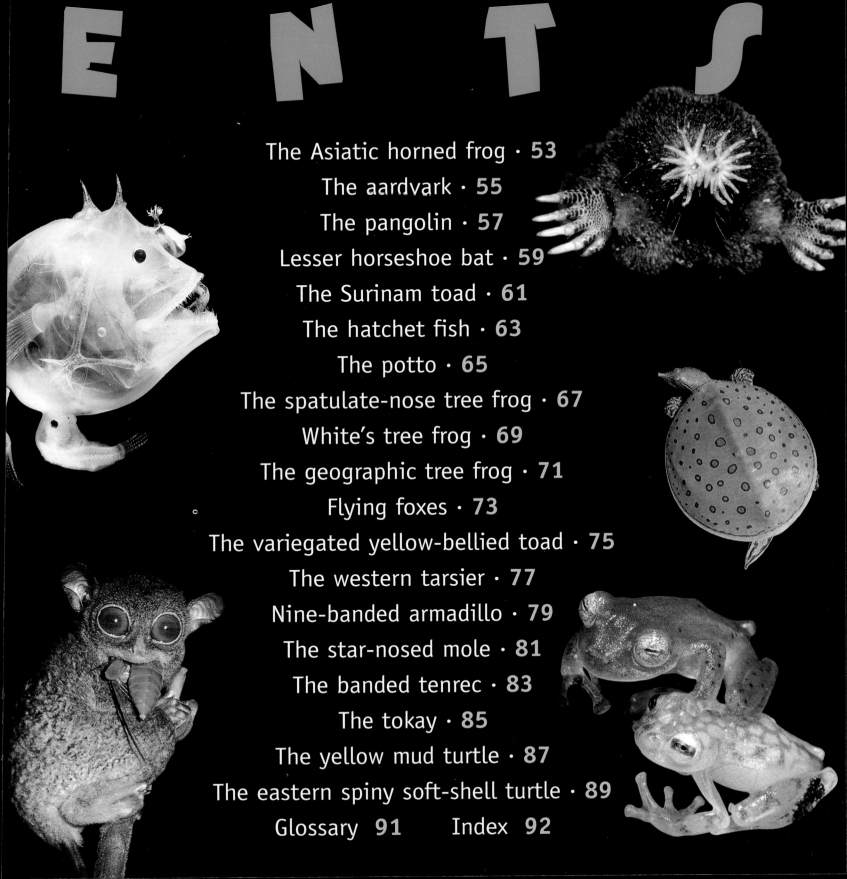

The axolotl

Is it a tadpole? Or is it a frog? The axolotl is a strange-looking creature, half fish and half frog, which is quite rare today. It is, infact, an amphibian. Axolotls can be black, brown or albino in colour. Some are such a translucent colour you can almost see through their tails.

The axolotl has two little eyes and a ruff of red plumes around its head. These plumes are its gills, and it uses them to breathe. The gills are filled with blood, and they extract oxygen from the water. The oxygen then passes to the creature's lungs. Carbon dioxide passes out in the opposite direction.

The axolotl's body looks as if it is in the middle of change, halfway between a tadpole and a frog. But most axolotls do not change. They keep this body shape all the way through their adult life.

The axolotl's name, which comes from an Aztec language, means 'water monster'. It lives all its life in water, although sometimes individual axolotyls lose their gills and metamorphose into land creatures.

DISTRIBUTION
THE AXOLOTL IS ONLY FOUND IN ONE PLACE IN THE WORLD: IN A HIGH-ALTITUDE LAKE IN MEXICO, CALLED XOCHIMILCO.

HABITAT
LAKE.

SIZE
UP TO 29 CM LONG.

DIET
PLANKTON, WORMS, INSECT LARVAE AND SMALL CRUSTACEANS.

DAUBENTONIA MADAGASCARIENSIS

The aye-aye

DISTRIBUTION
CERTAIN AREAS OF MADAGASCAR.

HABITAT
TROPICAL RAINFOREST, IN
MANGROVE FORESTS OR BAMBOO
THICKETS.

SIZE
BODY GROWS BETWEEN
35–45 CM LONG, BUT ITS TAIL
CAN BE UP TO 60 CM LONG.

DIET
GRUBS, BEETLES, BIRDS' EGGS,
YOUNG COCONUTS, MANGOES,
BAMBOO AND SUGARCANE HEARTS.

The first scientists to see aye-ayes did not know which animal group it belonged to. Eventually they classified it as part of the primate family, which also includes monkeys, apes and humans.

Aye-ayes once lived throughout northern Madagascar, off the coast of southern India. But this creature's strange appearance and frightening calls in the night made local people believe that any contact with it would lead to death. So many aye-ayes have been hunted and killed. Today, they are an endangered species and are only found in nature reserves.

The aye-aye only comes out at night. At dusk, it leaves its refuge and jumps between the branches of mangrove trees or bamboos, using its long, skeleton-like fingers.

Using its longest finger, the aye-aye taps on the bark of a tree to see if it is hollow, which means there may be insects inside. Then, with an ear up close to the tree trunk, the aye-aye listens carefully for the sound of insects gnawing wood. If in luck, it uses its sharp pair of front teeth to make a hole in the bark, slips its finger through the opening and pulls out a grub. As the aye-aye works, it gives little grunts of pleasure. But if anything approaches, it spits with anger and fear.

BABYROUSA BABYRUSSA

The babirusa

The babirusa is a wild pig that lives in the rainforests of Indonesia. It has wrinkled, hairless skin and incredibly long tusks, which grow up and backwards through its snout. In older males, the tusks can curve backwards so far that the tips meet the roots. Sometimes they pierce the jaw to form a complete circle.

Scientists believe the babirusa's tusks are used to deflect blows during attacks. The extraordinary shapes of these teeth are the source of fantastic myths and legends. The Indonesians say that the babirusa is capable of hanging itself from branches with its tusks.

Babirusas live in swamps and among reeds. Despite their bulky shape, they can trot quickly through thick undergrowth. They are also excellent swimmers. Babirusas can even cross short distances of sea to reach a neighbouring island.

Babirusas have been hunted for their meat and their tusks, which were made into bracelets and necklaces for tribal chiefs. This, and the loss of their rainforest habitat, means that babirousas are now an endangered species.

DISTRIBUTION
SULAWESI AND ITS NEIGHBOURING ISLANDS IN INDONESIA.

HABITAT
FORESTS AND THICKETS NEAR WATER.

SIZE
UP TO 1 METRE LONG, WEIGHING UP TO 100 KILOGRAMS.

DIET
ROOTS, BERRIES, BULBS, TUBERS AND LEAVES.

LINOPHRYNE

The deep-sea anglerfish

▼ A female anglerfish with the tiny male attached to her skin below.

The deep-sea anglerfish, with its wide mouth and round body, hovers deep in the oceans, at depths of over 2,700 metres.

This bizarre-looking fish has a luminous fishing line attached to its head, which glows in the dark and attracts prey. Scientists are still not sure how its fatal fishing line works. They think its light is caused by bacteria.

When prey comes near, the anglerfish opens its large, wide mouth, sucks its victim in and swallows it whole. Its round stomach can stretch to contain prey much bigger than itself.

The male anglerfish, which is only a tenth the size of the female, attaches himself to the skin of a female with his jaws and remains there permanently. Once he is attached, all his internal organs apart from his testicles weaken and become paralysed. A female anglerfish can collect a number of males throughout her lifetime.

DISTRIBUTION
ATLANTIC, PACIFIC AND INDIAN OCEANS.

HABITAT
DEEP IN THE OCEANS, AT DEPTHS OF OVER 2,750 METRES.

SIZE
UP TO 10 CM LONG.

DIET
SMALL INVERTEBRATES AND OTHER TINY ANIMALS.

Parson's chameleon

Chameleons look just like miniature dinosaurs. These curious reptiles have several amazing functions which help them catch their prey.

Their large, circular eyelids allow each eye to move separately and in all directions. This is ideal for watching out for prey while remaining absolutely still.

The chameleon's long, extendable tongue, with its sticky club at the end, can be slung out in an instant when prey comes close. The tongue retracts into a sheath that runs deep inside the chameleon's mouth.

The chameleon's feet and tail are ideally shaped for gripping branches. When not using its tail, it rolls it up in a coil.

But chameleons are most famous for their ability to change colour. Each species has a range of colours it can use. For example, some chameleons are totally lacking in shades of green, while others are missing the reds. Sometimes chameleons change their colour for camouflage. But it may depend on the time of day, or even just to reflect their mood.

DISTRIBUTION
MADAGASCAR. MOST OF THE OTHER 85 SPECIES OF CHAMELEON LIVE IN AFRICA, WITH A FEW OTHERS IN ASIA AND A SINGLE SPECIES IN EUROPE.

SIZE
UP TO 60 CM LONG.

DIET
LOCUSTS, SPIDERS AND OTHER INSECTS.

◀ A chameleon's tongue catches an insect.

The deep-sea viperfish

Viperfish have long, fang-like teeth. They live in the depths of the world's oceans, where it is very dark. In order to survive in their dark habitat, viperfish have evolved special ways of attracting mates so they can reproduce. Their bodies are also specially adapted to attacking and eating prey.

▲ *A viperfish photographed in ultraviolet light to show its luminous spots.*

On their bodies, rows of luminous green and red spots attract mates, and a filament attached to their backs lights up like a greenish lantern. During the day, these fish remain at depths of 450–2,800 metres. At night, though, in search of food, they swim up towards the surface.

Viperfish do not hesitate to attack prey larger than themselves. When it has decided to swallow something, the viperfish's jaws open and special muscles move its internal organs towards its tail. This means the fish's heart, aorta and network of arteries are pushed back from its mouth to leave as much room as possible for its dinner.

DISTRIBUTION
TROPICAL AND TEMPERATE WATERS OF THE ATLANTIC, PACIFIC AND INDIAN OCEANS.

SIZE
ABOUT 25 CM LONG.

DIET
FISH AND INVERTEBRATES.

CHLAMYPHORUS TRUNCATUS

The fairy armadillo

The fairy armadillo is a very rare creature. Its back is covered by a hard, protective covering, which is divided into segments. Beneath its segmented shield, the armadillo has thick white fur.

This unusual mammal lives in sandy and dry regions. At dusk, it leaves its burrow and takes short walks around bushes and cacti nearby. But it never leaves its burrow for long.

The armadillo's body is not designed for running. Its heavy paws, with their enormous front claws, are meant for digging. The armadillo digs to find its favourite food – earthworms and snails. As is digs, the armadillo drags the rest of its body behind, leaving a distinctive trail.

The South Americans are very fond of the armadillo. If they manage to trap one, they will try to keep it alive for as long as possible.

DISTRIBUTION
WEST-CENTRAL ARGENTINA

HABITAT
DRY SANDY PLAINS.

SIZE
BETWEEN 12–15 CM LONG.

DIET
SNAILS, EARTHWORMS AND ANTS.

ALYTES OBSTETRICANS

The midwife toad

DISTRIBUTION
WESTERN EUROPE
INCLUDING SPAIN.

HABITAT
WOODY AND CULTIVATED
LAND, RIVER BANKS, OLD
WALLS AND ROTTEN TREE
STUMPS.

SIZE
ABOUT 5 CM LONG.

DIET
INSECTS AND SMALL
INVERTEBRATES.

This tiny grey, olive or brown toad is named after the behaviour of the male when mating. After attracting the female using a high-pitched call, the male helps her lay a string of eggs by pressing her sides. When the eggs are laid, the male gathers them between his hind legs and fertilizes them. Then he wraps them around his legs and the couple of toads separate.

The male takes shelter with the clump of fertilized eggs still on his hind legs. He only leaves his hiding place at dusk, to search for food. If the weather is too dry, he carefully takes the eggs to a pond to wet them.

At the end of three weeks, the eggs are ready to hatch. The male toad takes them to a pond, plunges his rear legs in the water and the young tadpoles hatch. The male then gets rid of the empty egg cases.

As soon as he has delivered the eggs to the pond, the male midwife toad starts making his mating calls again, ready to start the cycle all over again.

The cane toad is one of the largest amphibians in the world. This species has often been deliberately imported into countries to help protect young plants. It helps farmers by eating the insects that damage their plants. The cane toad is fond of beetles, but also of birds and small rodents.

Glands located behind the cane toad's eyes secrete a poisonous substance, which strongly irritates the mucous membranes of other living creatures. It can be fatal to predators. Dogs and cats can die of poisoning after picking up one of these toads in their mouths.

Cane toads are also capable of shooting their poison over a distance of more than 30 centimetres. Even the eggs of cane toads are poisonous.

Cane toads are not afraid of humans, either. Sometimes they sit below street lamps and snap up insects that whirl around in the light.

DISTRIBUTION
FROM SOUTHERN TEXAS, USA, TO SOUTH AMERICA.

HABITAT
MARSHES AND PONDS.

SIZE
UP TO 23 CM LONG.

DIET
INSECTS, BIRDS AND SMALL RODENTS.

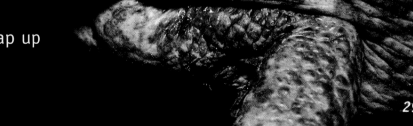

BUFO VIRIDIS

The European green toad

The European green toad has a distinctive patterned skin, with green patches and red dots. Like all toads, the green toad has three pairs of eyelids, one of which is movable and transparent. When the toad is underwater, the transparent eyelid covers the eyeball like the glass in a diver's mask. This gives the toad better underwater vision and protects its eyes.

Many ancient superstitions in Europe have been based on toads. Some people used to believe that toads drank milk from cows. Others thought they made wine go bad, and many thought they brought bad luck. But people also used to think that a toad placed under a pillow had the power to stop fevers. Sorcerers and magicians used toads in their magic potions.

DISTRIBUTION
EUROPE, FROM SOUTHERN SWEDEN TO GERMANY, ITALY, THE MEDITERRANEAN ISLANDS, NORTH AFRICA AND CENTRAL ASIA.

HABITAT
SANDY LOWLANDS.

SIZE
8–12 CM LONG.

DIET
INSECTS, SLUGS AND THE OCCASIONAL SMALL RODENT.

XENOPUS LAEVIS

The African clawed frog

The African clawed frog is named after the claws on its three inner toes. It uses these claws, which are webbed, to rummage through the mud at the bottom of ponds in search of food.

Seen from above, the frog looks like a pile of jelly. But its streamlined shape helps it swim as fast as a fish. As it swims, its short front legs act as probes, helping to detect food, while its powerful hind legs and webbed feet propel it along at great speed.

The African clawed frog mates in the water. The male makes a soft buzzing sound to attract a female, who is twice his size. Clawed frogs lay many eggs, around 10,000 each year. The eggs, enclosed in a transparent mucus, stick to vegetation and hatch seven days later. A large percentage of the tadpoles are malformed. These are eaten by their parents.

DISTRIBUTION
SOUTH AFRICA.

HABITAT
PONDS AND LAKES.

SIZE
BETWEEN 5–12 CM LONG.

DIET
INSECTS AND ITS OWN YOUNG.

TACHYGLOSSUS ACULEATUS

Short-beaked echidna

Echidnas are unique mammals because they lay eggs instead of fully formed young. They are round and fat, with a stiff coat covered in spines, which have given them their other name: spiny anteaters.

Echidnas' long beaks help them furrow the ground in search of insects. Their mouth is a narrow slit just big enough for a giant earthworm to slip through for dinner. Echidnas also possess powerful claws, which they use for burrowing into the ground to hide from predators.

When female echidnas lay an egg, they put it in a pouch on their stomach, a little like a kangaroo. Unlike kangaroos, however, the pouch is only temporary. The female grows it before she gives birth and it disappears afterwards.

After it hatches, the young echidna stays in its mother's pouch for six to eight weeks, drinking her milk. Female echidnas don't have breasts. Instead, a thick milk oozes over the hairs near her mammary glands. Her young laps up this milk while it is in the pouch, instead of suckling from her breasts.

▲ *A long-beaked echidna.*

◄ *A short-beaked echidna.*

DISTRIBUTION
SHORT-BEAKED ECHIDNAS: AUSTRALIA AND NEW GUINEA
LONG-BEAKED ECHIDNAS: NEW GUINEA

HABITAT
TALL GRASSES AND FOREST UNDERGROWTH.

SIZE
SHORT-BEAKED: 30–50 CM LONG.
LONG-BEAKED: 45–80 CM LONG.

DIET
SHORT-BEAKED: ANTS AND TERMITES.
LONG-BEAKED: EARTHWORMS

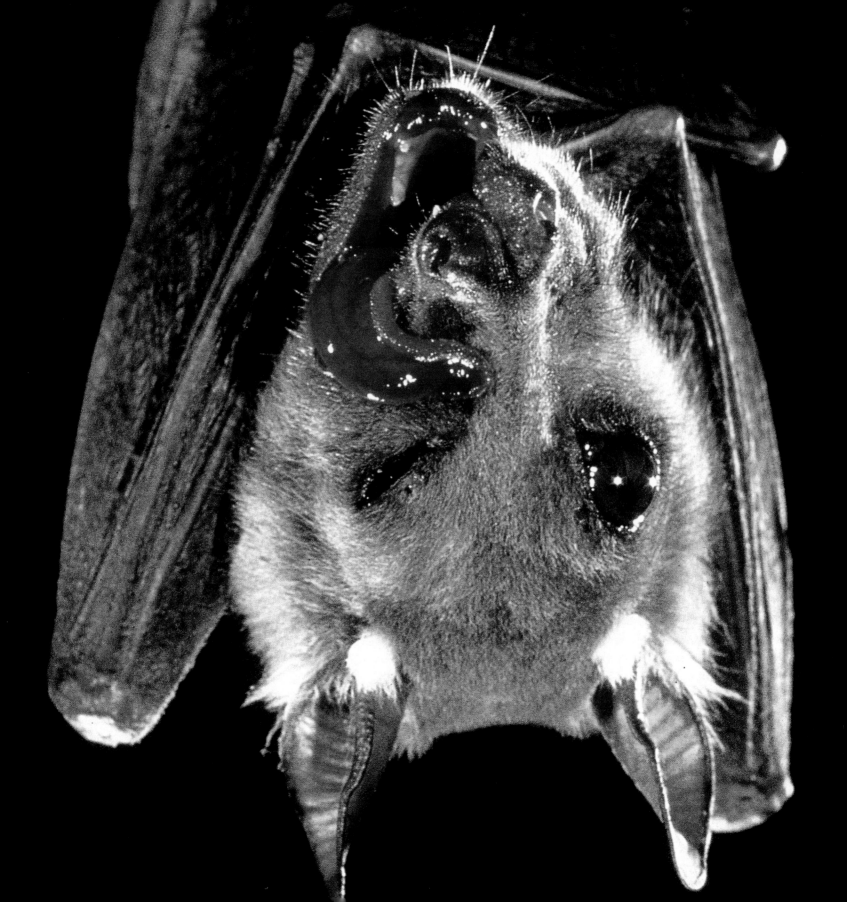

EPOMOPHORUS WAHLBERGI

Wahlberg's epauletted fruit bat

▲ *A fruit bat about to eat an apple.*

▲ *The mouth stretches around the apple.*

Bats are a strange type of mammal. They are the only mammals that can fly. Wahlberg's epauletted fruit bats have heads like tiny foxes, with long snouts and a soft fur coat. They spend their days amongst a small band of about fifeen other bats, hanging upside down from the tops of wild fig trees.

When darkness approaches, the bats leave their sleeping quarters and silently fly off towards orchards nearby. Most bats feed on insects, but fruit bats, as their name suggests, eat fruit. They use their excellent eyesight to spot the most promising apple trees and swoop down on them. After munching the fruit, they spit out the pulp and any fibre. Using one foot to hang from a branch, they use the other to clutch the fruit against their chests and devour it.

Some species of fruit bat do not eat the whole fruit, but content themselves with chewing on it like pieces of gum to suck out the juice.

DISTRIBUTION
AFRICA, FROM CAMEROON TO SOUTH AFRICA.

HABITAT
SCATTERED FORESTS OR SAVANNAH.

SIZE
ABOUT 14 CM LONG.

DIET
FIGS, MANGOES, PAPAYAS, AVOCADOS, GUAVAS AND BANANAS.

UROPLATUS FIMBRIATUS

The leaf-tailed gecko

Geckos are reptiles with excellent camouflage, which helps them blend in with their surroundings. Their bodies are covered by tiny coloured scales, and even their eyeballs are camouflaged by stripes.

There are 675 species of geckos. Some species are green and red like parrots. Others, like the leaf-tailed gecko, are the colour of bark or lichens. The leaf-tailed gecko has strips of sticky pads under its fingers and toes, which allow it to climb down smooth, vertical surfaces.

Geckos do not blink because their eyelids do not move. Instead, their eyelids are transparent and sit over the eyeball constantly like a contact lens.

The gecko's limbs have a fringe of scales. This means it can flatten itself against a tree-trunk without casting the slightest shadow and become invisible to its prey. If an insect passes by, the gecko flicks out its colourful tongue and catches it in a flash.

DISTRIBUTION
MADAGASCAR.

HABITAT
TROPICAL RAIN FORESTS, SWAMPS OR DESERTS.

SIZE
ABOUT 20 CM LONG.

DIET
FIGS, MANGOES, PAPAYAS, AVOCADOS, GUAVAS AND BANANAS.

SACCOPHARYNX LAVENBERGI

The gulper eel

The gulper eel lives in the depths of the ocean. It is named after the way it gulps down huge quantities of food. You can recognise one by its long, wavy body and its huge mouth.

The gulper eel isn't the fastest swimmer, but it is a champion eater. It can swallow prey bigger than itself thanks to its pharynx and its stomach, both of which it can expand to great capacities.

As it swims along, the gulper eel casually opens its mouth and gobbles the fish and crustaceans that get in its way. It can open its mouth to an angle of over 180º by tipping its head backwards. After a meal, all it has to do is tow its huge stomach beneath it. The gulper eel doesn't eat very often, but the size of its mouth and stomach mean that when it does eat, it makes up for it.

DISTRIBUTION
INDIAN, PACIFIC AND ATLANTIC OCEANS.

HABITAT
OCEAN DEPTHS OF 2,000 TO 5,000 METRES.

SIZE
BETWEEN 50 CM AND 2 METRES LONG.

DIET
EVERYTHING THAT PASSES ITS MOUTH, WHICH IS USUALLY OPEN!

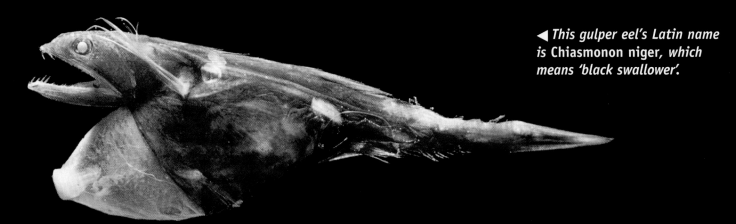

◄ *This gulper eel's Latin name is* **Chiasmonon niger,** *which means 'black swallower'.*

CERATOPHRYS ORNATA

Bell's horn frog

The body of Bell's horn frog is so swollen it looks as if it is about to explode! Its large mouth seems set in a permanent grin.

The horned frog will swallow anything that gets within reach. In the space of a few seconds, nothing remains of its victims but a foot or a tail hanging out of its immense mouth. Then they disappear completely.

This frog's body is patterned with bright-green, black and yellow, which helps camouflage it against its surroundings. Horned frogs lie in wait for prey by hiding among moss and leaves.

Their jaws are made like a steel trap and they have a constant appetite, snapping at anything that comes too close.

DISTRIBUTION
NORTHERN AND CENTRAL SOUTH AMERICA.

HABITAT
FOREST FLOOR.

SIZE
ABOUT 20 CM LONG.

DIET
SNAILS, MICE AND OTHER FROGS.

The glass frog

Glass frogs are tiny tree frogs. They are one of the smallest frogs on the planet. Glass frogs have shiny, translucent bodies. Their belly, in particular, is transparent. Through their belly you can see their stomach, the network of blood vessels, and even their beating heart. Scientists still don't know much about these amphibians because they are so tiny and know how to hide themselves perfectly among leaves.

They lay forty to fifty eggs in a jelly, which is stuck to the underside of leaves that overhang streams. One of the parents watches over the eggs, to protect them from being eaten by other frogs or beetles.

The pale-green patterns on the backs of glass frogs camouflage them so they remain unnoticed as they stay near their eggs. This protects them from the eyes of their predators, but it also helps them catch insects attracted by this pattern.

DISTRIBUTION
CENTRAL AMERICA, FROM COSTA RICA TO THE EQUATOR.

HABITAT
TROPICAL RAIN FORESTS.

SIZE
BETWEEN 2–3 CM LONG.

DIET
SMALL INSECTS, INCLUDING MOSQUITOES AND SPIDERS.

HYPSIGNATHUS MONSTROSUS

Hammer-headed bat

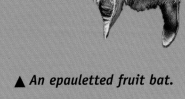

The hammerheaded bat is a type of fruit bat. It is one of the largest bats alive. The male of the species has a curiously shaped snout, with lips full of folds. This useful shape helps the bat wrap its lips around fruit and suck out the juice. But the snout has another reason, too. It acts as a type of megaphone, helping the male bat give out mating calls in the night.

At dusk, the males take off from their resting place with a powerful beating of wings. They settle on trees along the banks of waterways in the forest, and launch into endless singing competitions. Their voices sound like choruses of croaking, and are accompanied by more beating of their wings.

Above this chorus, females of the species slowly fly overhead, looking for a mate. Once the female bat has made her choice, she settles next to the male and they mate. Afterwards, the female takes off into the night.

▲ *An epauletted fruit bat.*

◀ *A hammerheaded bat (Hypsignathus monstrosus).*

DISTRIBUTION
AFRICA, FROM THE GAMBIA TO UGANDA, AND SOUTH TO ANGOLA.

HABITAT
MANGROVES OR PALM TREES.

SIZE
WINGSPAN RANGES FROM 70–95 CM.

DIET
MANGO OR SOURSOP JUICE.

LORIS TARDIGRADUS

Slender loris

DISTRIBUTION
SRI LANKA AND THE SOUTH OF INDIA.

HABITAT
RAINFORESTS.

SIZE
BETWEEN 18–26 CM LONG.

DIET
LIZARDS, SMALL BIRDS, EGGS AND INSECTS.

The slender loris is a night-time creature. It has the eyes of an owl, the feet of a mouse and a soft fur coat. The loris is a member of the primate family, which includes monkeys, apes and humans. Most primates are good climbers, and the loris's hands and feet are perfect for gripping branches of trees.

The loris was named after a Dutch word meaning 'clown'. It spends its days resting in hollow trees. When night falls, the loris climbs among the trees using extremely slow movements, looking for food.

Despite its slowness, the loris can be quite lively. It approaches prey with caution, but will suddenly grab it with both hands and munch on it. The loris's large, black eyes allow it to peer through darkness. It eats leaves, insects and eggs. Sometimes, it hunts lizards and nibbles a flower or two for dessert.

In India, there used to be a lot of superstitions surrounding the loris. People used to believe that its eyes could act as a love potion.

The matamata

The matamata is a semi-aquatic turtle, which means it lives both in and out of water. It is also known as the snake-necked turtle. The shell of the matamata is raised into peaks. Seen from above, its head looks flat and triangular. The skin covering the neck is rough, and dangles at the sides in a fringe. Some scientists think that the matamata's dangling skin attracts small fish, which is its prey.

The matamata is an agressive turtle. It waits for prey by lying submerged underwater in a river. It remains so still and for so long that algae can grow from its shell. Only its nose emerges at times from the water, like a snorkle.

When prey comes near, the matamata opens its mouth and throat. It sucks up the victim in one big gulp, as if it is taking a breath. The turtle takes its prey at such a speed that it is not easy to see with the naked eye. Researchers have had to film the action and run the film in slow motion to see what happens.

DISTRIBUTION
SOUTH AMERICA.

HABITAT
MARSHES AND SLOW-FLOWING RIVERS.

SIZE
UP TO 40 CM LONG.

DIET
FISH.

51

MEGOPHRYS MONTICOLA

The Asiatic horned frog

The Asiatic horned frog has raised pointed eyebrows, like horns, and a pointed nose. Its body is a coppery colour, ranging from brownish-yellow to dark-coffee, and is patterned like the veins of a leaf. The horned frog's colour, pattern and shape help to camouflage it perfectly against the vegetation of the rainforest floor, where it sits very still. Its horns are very soft and fragile, so it has to be careful not to bump them.

The horned frog uses its enormous mouth to swallow up small insects that walk on the surface of rivers. The frog is a night-time creature, and the tiniest light will scare it away.

This frog lays its eggs under hollow stones, in tree stumps or on pieces of old wood floating on water. For this reason, it chooses still waters, or rivers that flow very gently.

DISTRIBUTION
THAILAND, THE MALAY PENINSULA, BORNEO AND THE PHILIPPINES.

HABITAT
LAND NEAR RAINFOREST STREAMS.

SIZE
UP TO 12 CM LONG.

DIET
INSECTS.

The aardvark

The aardvark is a curious creature, with the eyes of a deer, a rabbit's ears, a pig's snout and the tail of a giant rat. It is so unusual that scientists have classified it in a family that includes only one species – its own.

The aardvark is a timid and solitary mammal. At nightfall, it nervously edges out of its burrow. From the entrance, it sniffs the air on the look-out for any danger. Then in two or three big leaps, it jumps out and up on to its legs.

The aardvark has poor vision, but it has very sensitive nostrils instead. Making the most of its highly tuned sense of smell, the aardvark walks along with its snout to the ground, sniffing out nests full of ants and termites. When it finds a nest, the aardvark uses its large claws to dig into it. Its giant tongue scoops out the ants and its mouth crushes them.

After a filling meal, the aardvark trots back to its burrow. This home is 2–3 metres long and ends in a type of chamber, where the aardvark sleeps. It sleeps in an unusual way. Instead of lying on its side, like most animals, the aardvark sleeps with its face down.

DISTRIBUTION
SOUTH OF THE SAHARA DESERT AND ACROSS THE WHOLE OF AFRICA.

HABITAT
FROM OPEN FORESTS TO SAVANNAH, WHEREVER THERE ARE TERMITE NESTS.

SIZE
FROM 1–1.65 METRES LONG.

DIET
ANTS, TERMITES AND WILD GOURDS.

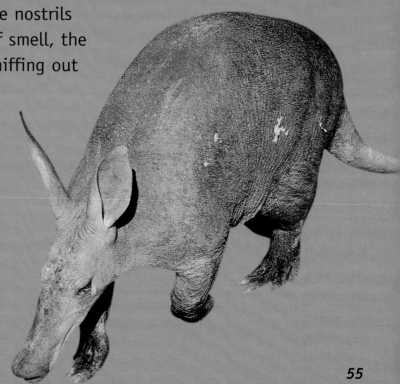

55

The Malayan pangolin

The Malayan pangolin looks like a giant pine cone on legs. Its body is covered by large overlapping scales, like a fish. The pangolin is the only mammal to be covered by scales, which are usually a feature of reptiles. If the pangolin is attacked, it rolls up into a tight ball, protected by its sharp scales. Because it is able to move each of its scales independently, the pangolin can wound its enemy by using them like razors.

The Malayan pangolin sleeps all day long, rolled into a tight ball, in the fork of a tree or lying in vegetation. Thanks to its long tail, the pangolin can also hang from branches. At nightfall, it wakes up to go in search of ants and termites.

To break into a termite nest, the pangolin leans on its hind legs and digs frantically with its long front claws. At the same time, it pokes its nose into the nest, causing panic inside. The pangolin has a giant tongue measuring up to 40 cm long, which it uses like fly paper to collect the termites and swallow them up.

DISTRIBUTION
THE MALAY PENINSULA, INDONESIA, INDOCHINA AND MYANMAR (BURMA).

HABITAT
TROPICAL RAIN FORESTS AND SAVANNAH.

SIZE
BETWEEN 75–80 CM LONG.

DIET
ANTS AND TERMITES.

RHINOLOPHUS HIPPOSIDEROS

The lesser horseshoe bat

DISTRIBUTION
EURORE, ASIA AND NORTH
AFRICA.

HABITAT
TROPICAL AND SUBTROPICAL
FORESTS, TEMPERATE
WOODLAND AND DESERTS.

SIZE
WINGSPAN MEASURES
BETWEEN 22–25 CM.

DIET
INSECTS.

The lesser horseshoe bat has a strange-shaped nose in the shape of a horseshoe. This 'noseleaf', as it is called, is actually a sophisticated tool. It helps the bat find its way through complete darkness, using a process called echolocation. This process is an alternative to using eyesight, which is why the horseshoe bat doesn't need big eyes.

During echolocation, the bat gives out high-frequency sounds using its larynx. Its noseleaf acts like a megaphone and magnifies the sounds, which bounce off obstacles and return to the bat's ears as echoes. The bat can use these echoes to make a 'sound picture' of its surroundings and help it find prey.

After a night of hunting insects, the lesser horseshoe bat finally flies home. In a fraction of a second, it turns a somersault mid-air, suspends itself and folds its wings. Mother bats close their wings around their young like a big coat. The lesser horseshoe bat hibernates from October to March each year, usually in a cave or crevice.

The Surinam toad

The Surinam toad has such a flat body that it looks as though it has been run over by a steam roller! Its head has tiny, star-shaped ears on either side of it.

When about to mate, the male Surinam toad grabs a female by her hind legs and the skin on her back swells up like a pillow. The eggs (between 40–100) are laid and fertilized during a sequence of amazing acrobatic somersaults.

The couple become entwined together, the male on top of the female, and turn somersaults in the water. When the two of them have their backs turned downwards, some of the eggs laid by the female fall on the male's belly, where they are fertilized. As the couple turn upright again, the eggs slip on to the female's back. After a few more turns, the fertilized eggs implant themselves in the skin of their mother's back.

After about ten weeks, the young begin to emerge, sometimes an arm, sometimes a leg, sometimes a head swallowing a water flea as it swims by. The young finally leave their home after 77–132 days.

DISTRIBUTION
NORTHERN PART OF SOUTH AMERICA, FROM VENEZUELA TO BRAZIL AND PERU.

HABITAT
RIVERS AND STREAMS.

SIZE
BETWEEN 15–20 CM LONG.

DIET
INSECTS, SLUGS, SNAILS, MICE, BIRDS AND YOUNG SNAKES.

61

ARGYROPELECUS

The hatchet fish

In the depths of the oceans, there is not enough light for plants to grow, and without plants, there is no food for fish. There is also enormous pressure at depth, which is equivalent to great weights pushing on an object from all sides.

For a long time, scientists believed that nothing could live at great depths in the oceans. But in these cold, black waters there are fish, often luminous like neon signs.

The hatchet fish has a silvery body, completely compressed, with small pearly eyes. These features help make the fish hard to see because its sides reflect other objects like mirrors. Predators find it hard to recognize the hatchet fish.

The hatchet fish's belly releases chemical substances, which give out a dim light tinged with blue. This light allows different species of hatchet fish to recognize each other. It also breaks up the fish's silhouette to make it harder for its predators to see it.

During the day, the hatchet fish lives at depths of 400–600 metres. But to eat, it has to swim up to the surface at night.

DISTRIBUTION
ALL THE OCEANS, EXCEPT THE POLAR SEAS.

HABITAT
DEPTHS OF BETWEEN 400–600 METRES.

SIZE
ABOUT 7 CM, SMALLER THAN A SARDINE.

DIET
TINY CRUSTACEANS.

The **potto**

DISTRIBUTION
WEST-CENTRAL AFRICA.

HABITAT
DEEP RAINFORESTS AND
WOODS.

SIZE
BETWEEN 30–40 CM LONG.

DIET
INSECTS, SNAILS, LEAVES
AND FRUITS.

One of the most amazing things about the potto is its almost human-like hands. They have a very large thumb and fingers with nails.

The potto also has two toes with sharpened claws, which it uses for defence. At the back of its neck, four of the potto's vertebra extend through the skin into points. If attacked, the creature can wound the agressor by tucking its chin into its chest. The bumps in the potto's neck can also be used as grips. Pottos attach them to tree branches when they want to fall asleep.

Potto couples mate face to face, which is quite rare in mammals. No other mammals do so except orangutans, bonobos and humans.

Young pottos are born in January or February. They are covered in silvery-white fur, and are usually so well-hidden in their mother's fur that it is very difficult to see them.

65

TRIPRION SPATULATUS

The spatula-nose tree frog

Unlike certain toads, tree frogs do not have poisonous venom to use against predators. They have a different form of protection instead.

The spatula-nose tree frog has a bony plate under its skin, and a nose like a duck's beak, which it uses for protection. When predators come close, the frogs take shelter in holes and use their heads to block the entrance. These small, nocturnal tree frogs from Mexico survive by hiding themselves in low vegetation, or in hollow trees.

During the dry season in Mexico, spatula-nose tree frogs remain quite inactive. But when the rainy season begins, from June to October, they spring into action.

During the rainy season, the tree frogs find mates and lay their eggs in fields and ditches flooded by heavy rains. They can even be found in the streets of Mexican cities.

DISTRIBUTION
WESTERN MEXICO.

HABITAT
VEGETATION OR HOLLOW TREES.

SIZE
UP TO 10 CM LONG.

DIET
INSECTS.

HYLA CAERULEA

White's tree frog

DISTRIBUTION
AUSTRALIA AND NEW
GUINEA.

SIZE
ABOUT 10 CM LONG.

DIET
AN INSATIABLE APPETITE
FOR FLIES, BUTTERFLIES,
EARTHWORMS AND
CATERPILLARS.

White's tree frog is perfectly adapted to living in trees. Its fingers and toes have sticky suckers on the ends, which allow the frog to grip tree branches. The inner finger and toe of each limb can move independently, like a thumb. Using its thumbs and its suckers, the frog can jump from bough to bough, even sticking to the underside of large leaves.

White's tree frog can also change the colour of its body depending on differences in light, humidity and even its mood. Its body is normally almond green. But if the frog leaves the sunny surface of a leaf for a cooler, shadier place, its body changes to beige. The ability to change colour helps camouflage this tree frog, to hide it from predators.

White's tree frog is often found in letterboxes, bathrooms, and even in toilet cisterns in Australia and New Guinea. From spring until autumn, the male frog sings a mating song, which sounds like "goo-groo-groo", sung louder and louder.

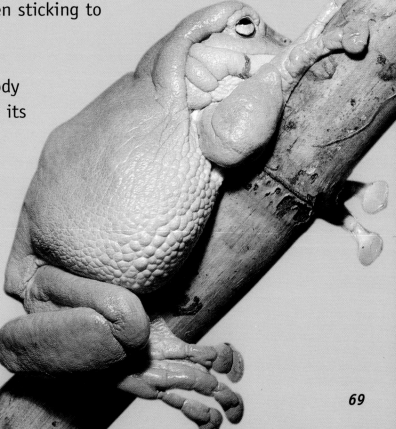

HYLA GEOGRAPHICA

The geographic tree frog

The geographic tree frog is a master of disguise. Its grainy skin has a brown leaf pattern and its body is so tiny that the frog can flatten itself against large leaves to hide from predators.

This tree frog can even camouflage its eyes. Instead of rust-coloured eyeballs, the frog can make them a type of net pattern, which makes them blend better into the surroundings.

The geographic tree frog sits in vegetation, waiting to gobble up insects that fly above the waterways and swamps. The frog has translucent, sticky suckers on the ends of its hands and feet which allow it to stick to vegetation and perch in bushes.

Near its thumbs, the frog has a swelling like a blister. This gives the male a good grip for holding the female during mating.

DISTRIBUTION
THE AMAZON BASIN IN GUYANA AND IN BRAZIL.

HABITAT
TROPICAL RAINFOREST.

SIZE
BETWEEN 4–5 CM LONG.

DIET
SMALL INSECTS AND INVERTEBRATES.

71

PTEROPUS

Flying foxes

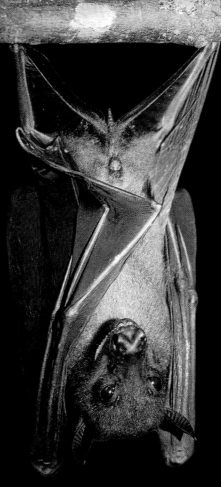

Flying foxes are fruit bats with faces a little like dogs. Their big nostrils and large eyes give them excellent smell and vision, which is essential for finding food.

Flying foxes spend their days hanging upside down from tree branches, resting. They gather in their hundreds, in groups called clusters. While resting, the bats wrap their leathery wings around themselves like a cape. When it gets too hot, they open up their wings and fan themselves.

When night falls the bats take flight, setting their course for fruit trees. Once they have found the trees, they crush the fruits between their teeth to suck out the juice, carefully spitting out the pits and seeds. Any fruits with soft flesh, like bananas, are swallowed greedily. Australian fruit bats swoop down on orchards and can destroy the harvest in a single night.

Once they have gorged themselves on fruit, the bats take an in-flight drink by skimming the surface of a lake or river. Finally, at dawn, they return home to their tree dormitories, gathering in their clusters for their daytime rest.

DISTRIBUTION
ASIA AND AFRICA.

HABITAT
TREES, CAVES, RUINS OR ROCK OVERHANGS.

SIZE
WINGSPAN CAN MEASURE UP TO 1.2 METRES.

DIET
MOSTLY FRUIT, BUT

BOMBINA VARIEGATA

The variegated yellow-bellied toad

The variegated yellow-bellied toad looks completely different from above and below. Its back is camouflaged by an earthy brown colour. But its belly is brightly coloured with yellow, blue and orange. This toad is also the only creature with heart-shaped pupils.

The yellow-bellied toad spends its days hidden under stones or tree stumps. At night, it leaves its hiding place and floats on the surface of water nearby. If the toad is attacked, it quickly turns on to its back and folds its front legs behind its back so they are out of sight. Its brightly coloured belly warns predators that it is poisonous. If the predator takes no notice, the toad can produce a white foam that smells like garlic. The foam irritates the mucus membranes in the nose and throat of the attacker, which usually makes it beat a hasty retreat.

DISTRIBUTION
WEST, CENTRAL AND SOUTHERN EUROPE.

HABITAT
STAGNANT WATERS RICH IN VEGETATION.

SIZE
4–5 CM LONG.

DIET
EARTHWORMS AND MOLLUSCS.

The western tarsier

DISTRIBUTION
THE ISLANDS OF SUMATRA AND BORNEO, IN INDONESIA.

HABITAT
UNDERGROWTH AND FORESTS.

SIZE
BETWEEN 9–16 CM LONG, BUT ITS TAIL MAY EXTEND UP TO 27 CM.

DIET
INSECTS, LARVAE, LIZARDS AND SMALL BIRDS.

Tarsiers are members of the primate family, which includes chimpanzees, monkeys and humans. Scientists believe that tarsiers allow us a glimpse of the past, because their behaviour is similar to the very first primates that lived, over 50 million years ago.

Tarsiers have huge eyes, but they only see well at night when their pupils dilate. In the daytime, when their pupils are just tiny dots, they cannot see much at all. Instead, they have to rely on their ears to sense danger, turning their heads very slowly in the direction of any noise.

The most unusual thing about tarsiers is their ability to turn their heads up to 180 degrees so they can see backwards. This caused superstition among the local tribes of Borneo, who were once headhunters. It was thought that if a man came across a tarsier on his way to war, he might lose his own head instead.

DASYPUS NOVEMCINCTUS

The nine-banded armadillo

Armadillos are covered with protective bony plates topped with horn. The nine-banded armadillo has nine movable, jointed plates. Its head is protected by a type of helmet, and its whole body is scattered with thick, coarse bristles.

If attacked, the armadillo rolls up into an almost perfect ball of body armour. Sometimes, it does not close up its body completely, but waits for a predator to stick its nose into a crack before giving it a pinch.

The armadillo has strong claws which it uses to dig its burrow, where it rests during the day. At night, the armadillo wanders along, poking its nose into the ground looking for food. It has a long, sticky tongue to scoop up insects and produces so much saliva that it has a special reservoir where it is stored.

The armadillo's greatest enemy has long been humans. Native American Indians roasted the creature in its shell before eating its flesh.

DISTRIBUTION
NORTH, CENTRAL AND SOUTH AMERICA.

HABITAT
FORESTS, GRASSLANDS OR SEMI-DESERTS.

SIZE
BETWEEN 40–50 CM LONG.

DIET
INSECTS, SPIDERS, SMALL REPTILES, FROGS AND EGGS.

The star-nosed mole

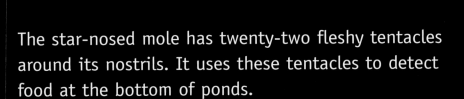

The star-nosed mole has twenty-two fleshy tentacles around its nostrils. It uses these tentacles to detect food at the bottom of ponds.

The star-nosed mole is also different from other moles because it is aquatic, which means it spends time in water as well as underground. It uses its front legs as paddles to swim. The mole digs tunnels in humid, marshy soils. Many of the tunnels end directly in water.

Day and night, summer and winter, the star-nosed mole crosses the countryside just below its surface, diving, swimming underwater and sometimes even under ice.

Female star-nosed moles produce a litter of between two and seven young moles between April and June each year. Their young are born with their own miniature nose stars.

DISTRIBUTION
SOUTH-EASTERN CANADA AND THE NORTH-EASTERN USA.

HABITAT
DAMP SOILS OF RIVERBANKS, LAKE SHORES, MARSHES AND WET FIELDS.

SIZE
BETWEEN 10–12 CM LONG.

DIET
EARTHWORMS, INSECTS, CRUSTACEANS AND SMALL FISH.

81

HEMICENTETES SEMISPINOSUS

The banded tenrec

Tenrecs are a very unusual type of hedgehog, which live in Madagascar. The tenrec's fur is mixed with very fine, pointed spines.

When threatened, the tenrec can make the spines on the back of its neck and the middle of its back vibrate, which makes a kind of rattling sound to warn off predators. If the predator takes no notice, the spines can detach themselves and stick into its skin.

Tenrecs also rattle their spines to communicate with other tenrecs as they look for food. The people of Madagascar say that when a tenrec finds a worm, it performs a kind of dance accompanied by a rattling of its spines to alert its companions.

All night long, families of tenrecs look for insects, poking their long noses under leaves and soil, sniffing for the smell of earthworms. When they find a worm, the tenrecs swallow it up on the spot. If they catch a big one, they hold it down with one foot and tear it to pieces. Tenrecs are so greedy that they often vomit after their meal.

DISTRIBUTION
MADAGASCAR.

HABITAT
UNDERGROWTH OR AT THE EDGE OF FORESTS.

SIZE
BETWEEN 15–20 CM LONG.

DIET
WORMS, SLUGS AND INSECTS.

GECKO GECKO

The tokay

The tokay is a type of gecko, or lizard. Like the leaf-tailed gecko and White's tree frog, it has sticky pads on its toes which make it a good climber. They allow it to walk up vertical walls and even upside down across ceilings.

Many tokays live near or even in houses in eastern Asia. They are very useful to people because they eat insects at night that would otherwise bother sleepers.

Female tokays spend the night making blowing sounds, while the males try to impress the females with loud, barking cries. But the males only bark in the mating season. This starts in December and reaches a peak between March and May. In this period, the tokays shout themselves hoarse trying to outdo each other. Then in June, they calm down and only bark occasionally until December.

In the mating season, the female tokay lays two eggs with sticky shells, which harden when they come into contact with the air. The eggs are attached to a vertical surface and are impossible to remove without breaking.

DISTRIBUTION
EASTERN ASIA.

HABITAT
NEAR AND INSIDE HOUSES.

SIZE
ABOUT 28 CM LONG.

DIET
COCKROACHES, MICE AND LIZARDS.

KINOSTERNON FLAVESCENS

The yellow mud turtle

The yellow mud turtle likes to stay at the bottom of marshes, or on the beds of slow-moving rivers. It buries itself in a sticky layer of mud made from decomposing plants. This species of turtle is so shy that people rarely see it.

The yellow mud turtle has a jointed breastplate below its belly, with front and back panels moving on hinges. These panels allow the turtle to close up its shell like shutters, completely protecting itself against attack.

Mud turtles spend their days lounging in their mudbaths, feeding on small aquatic animals, molluscs, dead animals and sometimes even the mud itself. Turtles have no teeth. Instead, they use the sharp edges of their jaws to tear food. Sometimes they swallow small pebbles to help grind their food.

The mud turtle will only leave the water to lay its two eggs. The eggs have very fragile shells, so the turtle lays them in a nest made out of rotting plants.

DISTRIBUTION
NORTH AMERICA, FROM ILLINOIS AND NEBRASKA TO TEXAS AND INTO MEXICO.

HABITAT
MARSHES OR SLOW-MOVING RIVERS.

SIZE
BETWEEN 9–16 CM LONG.

DIET
TADPOLES, WORMS, INSECTS AND FISH.

TRIONYX SPINIFERUS

The eastern spiny soft-shell turtle

Soft-shelled turtles have soft, leathery shells instead of hard shells. Their shells have air pockets inside them, which make them lighter and helps them swim. The shells are also a flatter shape, which makes it difficult to see the turtles at the bottom of ponds. This helps them hide from predators.

The eastern spiny soft-shelled turtle has a shell circled by one or two thin, dark rings and scattered with spots. The turtle has long nostrils like a snorkel, and a long neck which it can extend and retract. When the turtle retracts its neck, it folds up into an 'S' shape under the opening of its shell.

This turtle's long neck and nostrils allow it to breathe while its body stays underwater. But the water has to be shallow enough for the turtle to rest on the bottom while its nostrils poke above the surface. So its favourite waters are shallow creeks, ponds and streams. If the waters dry up, the turtle will bury itself in the mud until the following rainy season.

DISTRIBUTION
NORTH AMERICA, FROM CANADA TO FLORIDA, AND WEST TO COLORADO.

HABITAT
CREEKS, PONDS AND STREAMS.

SIZE
BETWEEN 15–45 CM LONG.

DIET
FISH, INSECTS, CRAYFISH AND MOLLUSCS.

GLOSSARY

Aorta The main artery of the body carrying blood from the heart.

Aquatic Growing or living in or near water.

Arteries Tubes carrying blood in the body, usually coming away from the heart.

Bacteria A group of microscopic organisms. Bacteria are the largest group of living things.

Camouflage The natural colouring of an animal which helps it blend in with its surroundings.

Classified Identified as belonging to a certain group. Classification is a system used by biologists of grouping living things together.

Crustaceans Invertebrates with jointed legs and two pairs of antennae. Woodlouse are crustaceans.

Dilate Get bigger.

Endangered species A group of animals or plants that is at risk of extinction.

Fibre Tough threads in animal or plant flesh.

Gills Organs used to breathe underwater.

Gourds A fleshy, large fruit with a hard skin.

Imported Brought in to a country.

Invertebrates Animals without a backbone.

Larynx Voicebox.

Larvae The young of animals which completely change their body shape when they grow into adults. Tadpoles are larave of frogs.

Lichens A type of plant that grows on rocks, tree trunks, roofs and walls, usually coloured green, grey or yellow.

Metamorphose Change shape.

Mucous membrane A lining of parts of the body which produces a slimy substance, for example, inside the human nose.

Nocturnal Only active at night.

Pharynx The part of the body just behind the nose and the mouth.

Predators Animals that kill and eat other animals.

Prey An animal that is killed and eaten by another animal.

Pupil The circular opening in the centre of the eye.

Rodents Mammals with sharp incisor teeth used for gnawing, such as mice.

Saliva Liquid supplied to the mouth to help eat food.

Species A small group within a larger group in the animal or plant kingdoms.

Soursop An evergreen tree with a large, juicy fruit.

Vertebra Segments of the backbone.

Wingspan The width between the tips of a pair of wings.

91

◀ *The eye of Rhacodactylus chahoua, a type of gecko.*

INDEX